The Successful Interview

2nd Ed. Why Should We Hire You?

Steve Williams

i

CONTENTS

INTRODUCTION

Are you ready to land your dream job and start making money today?
You're about to discover how to walk into your job interview and leave with a smile, you've got the job! Facing potential employers and undergoing question after question can be a daunting task. You sit there nervously wondering if you are answering everything correctly or if they even like you. Many people go to interview after interview focusing on all the wrong things with no one to tell them what exactly to do or say.

The truth of the matter is if you are having trouble with interviews and getting hired, it is because you are lacking effective techniques and strategies and have not yet been trained on what to do and say during your interview. This book has step by step advice that will help you land that dream job you've always wanted.

Thanks for buying this book; I hope you enjoy it!

CHAPTER 1 - TRULY UNDERSTANDING YOUR TARGET

Everyone dreams about the ideal job, one that is best suited for their skill set and allows them the opportunity to continually be challenged at work and overcome problems in a meaningful fashion. And yet, far too few people truly understand all of the steps necessary to getting that dream job. Thankfully, there are seven steps that you can follow to land your dream job.

This eBook will teach you to define your target first and foremost. Don't just have the title for your dream position or the company where your dream job should exist in theory. Instead, list everything from your title and your responsibilities to the department you will work in and the support you will be offered, all the way to the compensation and benefits you should receive. This eBook will show you how to know your value, which is really better defined by taking the time to analyze roadblocks you have previously faced in your career and how your skills were applied to overcome those barriers and achieve results. You should do much more than simply tell your potential hiring manager what you have to offer. Instead, you should generate excitement about what things you can bring to the table in a tangible way by really demonstrating qualitative and quantitative results you have achieved in the past.

This eBook will show you how to do that by sharing convincing stories and compelling statements about not only what it is you do currently but what you can do with this company and how you will do it. The best way to show anyone what you can do for them is through a story. The story should be something that covers a previous situation where you brought results to the company. This is important because it conjures an immediate thought process within the hiring manager as to how results like that would have benefited their company. You will also learn how to create a strong resume that has a professional image. You will want to pass the 10-second test, avoid any mistakes, and present a valuable contribution to the reader, such that they cannot help but be impressed. You will learn how to use all communication as a marketing weapon so that your cover letter functions as more than mere wrapping paper around your resume and, instead, helps you to build a network of opportunities with others. In the end, you will also learn how to create rapport with your interviewer by asking insightful questions early on rather than waiting until the end and by using the interview opportunity to create a dialogue between the two of you or however many people are present, rather than just a question and answer session. Finally, this eBook will show you how to focus on the challenges you have overcome in the past, and how you can convey the application of your skills in these endeavors to the interviewer. You want to show that you can do more than just completing mundane, routine tasks, but that you can also apply critical thinking.

Defining Your Target

When you set out to land your dream job, you need to know the specifics about that job. Most people know what their "dream" employment would be, but they cannot answer additional questions about the specifics of it.

If your goal is to be CEO, know more than the title.
You should list the following information:

- What is the title you want?
- What duties and responsibilities would you want?
- In what department is your role?
- To whom would you report in this dream job?
- What support would you have at your new job?
- If you are in a managerial position, how big should your staff be?
- What levels of people would report to you?
- Geographically, where would this job be located?
- How much travel would be required of you on a local, regional, national, and even international level?
- In what industry is your new job located?
- How large is the company you want to work for and what is it about the size of the company that you find the most appealing?
- How would you describe the company culture?

- Can you list any current companies you are interested in? What is it about that company that attracts you to them?
- What is your required compensation and benefits versus the current market?

These should all be questions you can use to define your dream job. You want to remain flexible at all times in the opportunities that present themselves to you, but by sticking to this list of information, you can stay on track when pursuing your dream job.

Many job seekers hesitate to focus their search because they want to be open to "whatever is available". They talk to hiring managers but are fearful of being honest and specific about what it is they are good at or interested in because they worry that some unspecified job opening might be up for grabs, and they don't want to miss that.

This is an attitude where one waits for someone else to provide an indication of the "right" answers. For example: Sitting in a hiring manager's office and being vague about your skills until the manager mentions a new opening and the specific skills it requires, then catering the response to meet that job.

But, what many people fail to realize is that this hesitation and lack of specifics makes people skeptical of hiring the person because it paints the picture of someone far from passionate or qualified. Potential employers like focus, and they like to see that someone is a good fit for the job and passionate about what they do. Consider this: If you are passionate and make immediate claims about what it is you can do, you will impress the hiring manager so much that even if you do not fit their requirements precisely, they will be more willing to explore alternative positions or even create a position for you.

When you are defining your target, you also want to make sure that the target you're describing is the right target. The greatest success will come from first aligning what it is you do best with the things you love. If you land your dream job, you can set yourself apart from everyone else, but it is only after you have determined where your skill set and the things you love intersect that you should concentrate on finding out how to achieve your life goals from that area. You need to know, first, what your skills are and what you love to do before you figure out how to satisfy all of your life goals. You want to find a target that matches your passions and your skills, and after you have done that, you can worry about how to make that fit into your life goals. But this is truly one of the defining concepts behind a dream job.

CHAPTER 2 – KNOWING YOUR VALUE

One important aspect of finding the dream job is to take personal time to reflect and analyze what skills you bring to the table. You will not be able to convince anyone else of your value if you cannot make a list of what things you have accomplished and what you gained from those accomplishments.

Take a moment to ask yourself what barriers you have overcome in the course of your career, and not only what they were, but also why the roadblocks were there, why the project was important, who suggested the project, and how you applied your skills and your experience to overcome the roadblocks. Add the challenges you faced personally in getting those results and be sure to generate excitement about what you did accomplish and what you can achieve for this company. This will reach the person listening to you on an emotional level and cause them to think critically about what results like that might mean for their business, too.

Your goal here is to be clear about the results you produced for your employer. How you can help redesign a system for your dream company such that you reduce their errors, and the amount of resources used will be more appealing to potential employers compared to the fact that you have experienced redesigning systems?

In other words, don't just tell someone that you are good at something, like product management. Instead, use a story to explain how once you delivered a product one month ahead of time and gained an additional $100,000 in revenue for your company.

This is not only intended to give an example of your work, but it will also show that you can think strategically and that you hold potential for leadership inside of you. The more in touch you are with your work and what it means for the company, the more likely it is that you will be perceived as someone who puts in a little extra effort to meet requirements.

CHAPTER 3 – HAVE A STRONG RESUME WITH A PROFESSIONAL IMAGE

Once you have the stories that indicate your value, review them carefully. Take some time to reflect upon the solutions that you brought to your previous employers and all of the different problems you have solved throughout your career. Focus on those in every piece of communication you have, including your pitch, your resume, and your cover letter. Never answer the question "What do you do?" in a literal fashion. Instead, frame that question into "Why should the company pay you a high salary?". In other words, you want to provide solution-oriented examples that show the employer why you are worth all of your compensation and benefits. You should have a compelling statement about what you want to do. No one will be impressed with a generic statement about what job you want, but they will be impressed with a problem statement that shows what you've been doing in your career and how you can apply that to this new job. Just indicating that you measure the financial impact of events is not effective because it's very vague and no one will necessarily know what you're talking about and even if they do know, they also know you didn't say very much. But if you explain that you make sure to deliver products that are profitable and marketable, you will garner a great deal more attention because people see that you can engage with your company and the audiences therein.

You need to have an outstanding resume. Your resume needs to grab the attention of anyone and everyone. If you are looking for a management level dream job, make sure that you state something other than "looking for a management level position that will allow me to use my skills and talents in leadership and mentoring to improve a company's efficiency and energize my career." This is a common mistake. This type of statement focuses more on what's important to the individual and not what is important to the hiring manager. Whoever is hiring you will not care about solving your problems, only how you can solve their problems. They won't care about building up your career for you by giving you this job. They are only interested in what you can do to solve their problems. So to grab their attention, you should answer the following questions:

Does your resume produce a sharp, professional image?

Does your resume pass a 10-second test?

Will your resume prove that you can deliver?

A sharp, professional image draws an immediate conclusion about the potential quality of the work you can provide. Consider this resume much like a sales brochure where you need to avoid any errors or sloppiness or even a slight issue with the margins. If you claim that you have outstanding communication skills, it will only make it that much worse when the reader finds a spelling error or grammatical error. And at that point, you have proven that they cannot trust your word, and there is no reason that they should hire you. Your resume needs to communicate that you are professional and that you not only took the time to write out the different bullet points but that you also had someone else proofread it, and then you proofread it just to make sure that everything was on the up and up.

The 10-second test is something that every person should consider when they're building their resume for their dream job. All hiring managers and recruiters have to look at hundreds of resumes for any potential job opening, and they will not have time to read each one. Most of them are going to look at any resume for no more than 10 seconds before they have determined whether or not you are a possible candidate. This means that your objective is to tell the reader what you bring to the table and what problems you can solve for their company right away. This should be done within 10 seconds of reading the resume

Your resume should prove that you can deliver results. Demonstrate that you can produce results that are relevant to the company. Don't give them a simple laundry list of what duties you have completed and passed. There's no need to give them all the details about what it is you did at this particular juncture, but you should get straight to the results you achieved. No one pays an individual just to perform a duty. They pay you because of the results you can produce. Do not simply say that you are responsible for product management. Instead, under product manager, list the exact results you produced for the company in that position, such as delivering a new program under budget, completing a challenging project, making a company's procedure more efficient, turning an otherwise dissatisfied customer into a long-term customer, etc. If at all possible, include quantitative data or metrics. Do not just say that you increased efficiency for a company, but rather that you reduced runtime by 15%.

CHAPTER 4 – USING COMMUNICATION AS A MARKETING WEAPON TO BUILD A NETWORK OF OPPORTUNITIES

The term 'cover letter' is something that conjures the image of wrapping paper or an otherwise useless item that serves only to be unwrapped. But if you approach the cover letter with this attitude, it won't do you any good, and you will only waste your time. You need to look at your cover letter as a marketing letter, something that can be quite powerful. Yes, it is true that not everyone will read the cover letter, but they will notice whether or not it was included. And because it is typically part of your application file, it will be shared with anyone else you meet during the interview, and having a letter that was powerfully written can influence much more than you might think.

Think of all the marketing pieces you have received in your mailbox time and time again. Review your opinion of a brochure that arrived without a letter or something that was merely stuck in an envelope. It usually comes across as though it was a mass mailing and that the sender put forth no effort. And unless the cover of the brochure really jumps out and grabs your attention, it's probably going into the trash bin. But consider a brochure that has arrived with a poorly written cover letter. That seems to be worse in some way. Even if the brochure is well done, the cover letter being poorly written might cause you to question whether the company is capable of excellent service. But if you receive a brochure that is accompanied by a persuasive and personalized letter, you will be much more likely to consider the services of the sender. The reason for this is because you begin to draw the conclusion that they are a real professional because of the effort they put into a simple mailing.

It is this idea that you need to implement in your resume's cover letter.

When you apply for a particular job, you have to include your resume, but in some situations, a powerful letter might be all you need to convey strength. So, consider all of your emails and your cover letters as a marketing letter, something that you should approach with a new perspective.

In addition to this, you also want to build up your network of opportunities. When you are searching for your dream job, let everyone you know in on that fact. Let them know that you're looking for your dream job, what that dream job is, and why you would be an outstanding candidate. Now, you should not do this by simply sending a mass email to all of your friends or handing each family member a resume next time you see them. Do not come across as though you are asking them to help you find a job because if you do, it looks like you are asking them for a big favor, and it might make them hesitate to refer you, or they might assume that you are trying to impose upon them. You also put them on the spot. So, someone, who might sincerely want to help you, might feel awkward because of your many phone calls. So, even if you are calling just to catch up with a friend, they might wonder whether you are going to bring up the job matter and used the call just to be on the safe side. It also puts blinders on your friends and family and focuses their cognitive efforts solely on finding a job for you and whether they have an opening for you or know someone who has an opening for you. But this might mean you miss potentially influential contacts that might help you build up a connection and a network of opportunities.

If you are networking with your friends, never assume that they know what skills you bring to the table. Your friends and your previous coworkers probably have a mental idea of what it is you bring to the table based on their past dealings with you, but you need to make sure that they have a complete image. Draw them a clear picture of what it is you have to offer. Don't let people get off the hook simply by offering to send your resume to their hiring department. Thank them for their offer if they extend it, but try and have them introduce you to someone you can physically speak with. Don't just have your resume handed off into oblivion. Instead, focus on building a set of connections.

When you are networking, do it the right way. Avoid constantly being in a seller's mode, trying to get to as many people as possible. This is not networking. Networking is really about building relationships with people, and it is something that takes a great deal of time. Constantly meeting new people, but never cultivating a relationship with them will limit the meaningful opportunities you receive. You need to follow up on networking opportunities and try to build something rather than just moving from one networking event to another. You should be selective about your networking. You will not be friends with everyone, and you will not receive meaningful opportunities from everyone you meet. Develop relationships that are most likely to help you in the long-term. Allocate the time and energy you need to different events that would prove promising for your career. Focus on referrals to people who hold similar jobs to the one you want or who work in target companies.

CHAPTER 5 – BUILDING CONNECTION WITH YOUR INTERVIEWER

After creating your network of opportunities and crafting the perfect marketing brochure via your cover letter, you still have other tasks that need to be completed, and that begins with the interview. The interview is typically a question and answer session, but you want to make it your goal to build rapport with your interviewer. You want the interviewer to think of you as an individual they want on their team, someone they want in the office next to them, helping them to achieve company goals. Simply waiting to be asked a question and then answering that question does not convey this feeling to the interviewer. This approach just leaves you looking passive, far from someone ideal for a leadership position, and it will not impress any hiring manager. If you have questions, do not wait until the end of the interview to ask them. If you wait until the closing of the interview – when the interviewer asks, "Do you have any questions for us?" – then you have already missed out on your opportunity. Ask any insightful questions you have immediately because, at the end of the interview, your interviewer has already determined what they think of you and any impact that your questions might have had on them will be completely lost.

It is best for you to ask these questions regularly, throughout the course of the interview as they come to you. You want to make these queries flow seamlessly as though you are having a natural conversation with the interviewer, something that goes both ways. You want the interviewer to believe that working with you would be enjoyable and that having you on the team would help them to achieve their company goals. This does not mean that you should respond with a question to every question they ask because that becomes quite obvious and tedious. But every second or third query that is asked of you should be responded to with a question that fits into the natural flow of the existing conversation. This can be something like a clarifying question.

For example, if the interviewer asks you to clarify your strengths, your answer might be something to the effect that "I would have to say that one of my biggest strengths is my ability to deliver consistent results on time, see the bigger picture, and, of course, my persuasive presentation skills. Which of those skills would you like me to tell you about first?"

In answering their question like this, you keep them engaged, and you create a conversation rather than a boring, question-and-answer process. But at the same time, it also provides you with valuable insight as to what is most important to this company. If the first thing they asked to hear about is your persuasive presentation skills, then you know that this is perhaps one of the most important aspects.

Of course, you have to avoid over-thinking the questions that you were going to ask. Don't put energy into worrying about what questions you think the employer wants you to ask. Instead, focus on the information you personally require to determine if this particular position, company culture, or boss is someone you personally want to work with. Remember that this interview serves as an advantageous situation for you as well in determining whether this position is truly the best fit. Your dream job should be an ideal job, and if you get the feeling in the middle of the interview that this is not a company culture where you actually want to work, then it means that you have asked the right questions, and now you can turn your efforts to another position. You want to ask the questions that allow you to have a comfortable conversation and gain useful insight.

CHAPTER 6 – FOCUS ON YOUR CHALLENGES

During your interview, you need to focus on the challenges you have overcome in the past and how you were able to apply your skills to overcome those challenges. This is important because it shows that you will do much more than just complete a tedious and/or otherwise routine task, but that you will also apply your critical thinking skills in a very experienced manner. When you get into the interview, focus on previous challenges, the problems you solved for a former employer, or the challenges the current organization or hiring manager might be facing for which you offer the ideal solution.

Why do this?

Because the hiring managers will not be excited about hiring you just because you can complete a tedious daily task. They will want to hire you if they see that you are a solution to the challenges they are facing as a company. Companies are always facing a challenge. Otherwise, they wouldn't be looking to hire anyone new. The more you understand the issues they confront, the better you will be at communicating how you can solve their problem. People will not be impressed by the work you can do, but by the challenges you have overcome to get the work done. Anyone off the street can complete regular tasks, but not everyone can overcome the problems on the road to completing those tasks. If you truly do an outstanding job, you will make all challenges dissipate and leave the impression that everything was easy. This is why you have to provide accomplishment stories that draw upon the issues you overcame, issues that might not be known to many people within the organization.

It can be impressive to explain that you created a new application for commercial loans that included viability studies and market research. It might be even more impressive to indicate that your CEO recognized that new application as an avenue for large scale growth that has already provided $2 million in advanced commitments. This story describes exactly what you did, what you accomplished, and the measurable results. But what would make this story even more compelling is if you started a bit earlier and began the story by introducing the challenge that existed in the first place, the challenge that caused you to receive the assignment to create the new application in the first place. For example, you might begin the story by stating that your company wanted to go public, and they were a young company, but they had limited revenue streams, which made it tough for them to meet their goals. As a result, they needed to diversify, and they brought you in to create the new application for commercial loans. And from there, you could continue the story with the recognition received by the CEO, the growth it created, and the advanced commitments. By including the addition of the original challenge, you can improve the story and make your results seem all the more impressive.

With each project you finish, you want to highlight your accomplishments by starting with the key challenges you were originally facing when you made those accomplishments happen. Never assume that the hiring manager will know the problems you faced just because they read your resume. Also, never assume that you know the problems the hiring manager is facing simply because you read over their job description. If this is truly your dream job, they will probe deeply into the different challenges that the position in question might bring to the table; why those are challenges; what it means for the overall operation of the company; what it costs the business and why you are a powerful solution for the company.

In the end, everyone dreams about the ideal job, but far too few people truly understand all of the steps necessary to getting that dream job. Now, you have all seven steps needed to land the perfect dream job.

This eBook taught you to define your target first and foremost. Don't just have the title for your dream position or the company where your dream job should exist in theory. Instead, list everything from your title and responsibilities of the department in which you will work to the support you will be offered, and all the way to the compensation and benefits you should receive. This eBook showed you how to know your value, which is really better defined by taking the time to analyze roadblocks you have previously faced in your career and how your skills were applied to overcome those roadblocks and achieve results. You should do much more than simply tell your potential hiring manager what you have to offer. Instead, you should generate excitement about what things you can bring to the table in a tangible way by really demonstrating qualitative and quantitative results you have achieved in the past.

This eBook showed you how to do all that by sharing convincing stories and compelling statements about not only what it is you currently do but also what you can do with this company and how you will do it. The best way to show anyone what you can do for them is through a story. The story should be something that covers a previous situation where you brought results to the business. This is important because it conjures up an immediate thought process within the hiring manager as to how results like that would have benefited their own business as well.

You also learned how to create a compelling resume that has a professional image. You will want to pass the 10-second test, avoid any mistakes, and present a valuable contribution to the reader such that they cannot help but be impressed. You learned how to use all communication as a marketing weapon so that your cover letter functions more than mere wrapping paper around your resume and, instead, helps you to build a network of opportunities with others.

In the end, you learned how to create rapport with your interviewer by asking insightful questions early on rather than waiting until the end and by using the interview opportunity to create a dialogue between the two of you or however many people are present, rather than just a question and answer session. Finally, this eBook showed you how to focus on the challenges you have overcome in the past and how you can convey the application of your skills in these endeavors to the interviewer. You want to show that you can do more than just completing mundane, routine tasks, but that you can also apply critical thinking.

CHAPTER 7 - WHY INTERVIEWERS ASK CERTAIN QUESTIONS

Did you know that when you are being interviewed for a job, some questions are strategically asked, which depending on your answer, will determine whether or not you receive a job offer?

Many of these queries will be about your past, but let's face it, the interviewer really does not care to know all about your past; what they are trying to do is learn what your past behaviors are in order to predict future behavior.

We will go over, in a later chapter what specific questions are usually asked in an interview as well as how you should answer them, but it is important for you to understand exactly why questions are asked to ensure that you are answering them appropriately and not throwing yourself under the bus so to speak.

One very common question that an interviewer will ask is for you to tell them about yourself. They are not looking for a play by play life story here; what they are looking for, however, is to detect if there is something wrong with you. For example, if you are habitually late, you are going to blurt out something that will alert them to this flaw and will remove you from the pile of candidates.

Interviewers will often ask what type of work you are looking for. This is a fairly straightforward question; they simply want to know that you are looking for the type of work that they have an opening for. They are also trying to eliminate anyone that is not searching for that particular type of work. For example, if you apply to be a cashier, but it turns out you really want to be a manager instead, they are going to be able to tell this by the way you answer this specific question.

Some interviewers may ask you about your health; if there is an obvious health issue; or they may ask you how many days you missed or were late to your previous job. This is one of those questions that is risky depending on how it is worded but the interviewer is again trying to determine what your future behavior will be based on your past behavior. For example, if you tell the interviewer that you have an issue with being on time regularly or that you missed a lot of work due to various doctor appointments or for some other reason, they can pretty much guarantee that this pattern of behavior will continue if they hire you.

Often times, most interviewers will ask why you left your previous job, or they may ask how you got along with your former employer or coworkers. The reason that they want to know this is that they want to ensure that you are able to get along with those who are in authority and those that you will work with on a day to day basis. They are also waiting to see if you bad mouth your previous employer, one of the bosses or even another coworker.

If there are gaps in your work history, the interviewer is going to want to know about that as well. It is important for the interviewer to know that you are not going to decide that you want to quit your job and just walk out. When they see gaps in work history, they get the message that you do not have to have a job because you have survived without it in the past, and they need to know that the job is important to you and that you are going to do your best. Another worry that interviewers have when there are significant gaps in work history is that you are not the type of person that enjoys working, or that you are not really ready to enter the workforce.

Many times, you will find that you are over qualified for a job, and this is going to be apparent to the interviewer. They are going to ask you about this because they need to be reassured that you are not going to call for a bigger salary once you are hired. They also need to know that you are not just going to work for them until you are offered a better position at another company.

Interviewers are known to ask a potential employee to tell them about their weaknesses. This is for several different reasons. The first reason is that the interviewer wants to know if you are aware of your weaknesses. He wants to make sure that you understand which specific areas you need to work on, and he intends to know about your strengths as well so that he can ensure those strengths are used appropriately in your new role.

Asking a potential employee about a problem that they faced in a previous work environment and how they solved it is also a common question that you will be requested to answer during an interview. The interviewer is asking this question because they want to know if you are able to solve problems that present themselves in the workplace. With your answer, they are able to access your skill set and determine if you are able to think outside of the box when you are solving a problem.

Depending on the position that you are applying for, an interviewer may ask you how you would feel about firing someone. This does not mean that you are going to have to fire someone; it only means that the interviewer wants to know how you would handle making tough decisions and having tough conversations with your coworkers. When you answer this question, the interviewer is going to be able to tell if you are the type of person that puts the company's interest above your own or the other way around.

Many interviewers will also ask you how you feel about workplace romance. This is a way for the interviewer to understand if you have done your research and familiarized yourself with the company's policy on the subject as well as how lenient you will be if the topic were to arise. It also lets them know if you are the type of person that would take part in this activity. As I stated earlier, we will talk more about how you should respond to some of these questions as well as others later in the book, but it is important for you to understand that workplace romances are generally looked down on and should be avoided at all costs.

It is imperative for you to be prepared to answer any of the questions. It is also important for you to make sure that while the interviewer is trying to get you to blurt out some negative aspects about yourself, you should instead, stay focused on the positive aspects as well as the skills that you have, which will make you an asset to the company.

Put yourself in the interviewer's shoes. Would you want to hire someone like you to work for your company if they told you all of the negative things about them? Of course not, none of us would, but when you focus on the positive aspects as well as what skills you have, you are putting your best foot forward even if you know there are some areas that you need to work on.

If you are aware that you are habitually late for work, create a new habit of being 15 minutes early no matter where you are going, and soon you will break the habit of being late. If you know you miss a lot of days, make a goal of not missing any days for three months and once you reach that goal, reward yourself. You will find that suddenly, instead of having a habit of missing work, you are in the habit of being at work every day!

Just because you focus on the positive aspects of yourself does not mean that you ignore your shortcomings. Take note of them and start working to change them. Soon, you will acknowledge that your job is no longer a difficult job, but no matter what it is, it will be a career that you enjoy doing.

CHAPTER 8 - WHAT IS AN INTERVIEWER LOOKING FOR

You will probably find yourself wondering what the interviewer is looking for when they are interviewing you. You want to know how you can make them start liking you and how you can stand out from the rest of the applicants.

While you may feel that you are the only one searching for clues while you are in an interview, the truth is, the interviewer is actually doing the same thing. They are listening to your questions carefully, paying close attention to your body language, watching how you handle yourself during the entire process and trying to access what it would be like to have you working for them or with them.

Therefore, it is important for you to understand exactly what an interviewer is looking for so that when you leave the interview, you will know you have aced it.

The first thing that an interviewer is going to want to ensure is that you are actually answering the questions that are being asked. It is crucial for you to take the time to prepare for an interview and understand what the common questions are. It is also vital for you to practice your answers over and over again. However, during the interview, you really need to push everything else out of your head and listen to what the interviewer is really asking you, not what you think they are asking you or what you think they are going to ask you.

You do not want to go into an interview with a bunch of memorized answers that do not remotely come to answering the question that was asked, this is not how you get hired. While it is important to have some answers prepared, these are not going to help you at all if the interviewer asks a completely different question.

Make sure that you listen to the entire question and reply carefully but naturally as well. You do not ever want to cut the interviewer off before they are able to finish asking the question and quickly jump into some prepared answer that is meaningless to them.

You have to trust that you are going to be able to respond to the question in just the same way you would if it was a friend or family member asking the question. You want to make a good connection with the interviewer because that is one of the things they are looking for, and you can do this by being conversational.

The next thing that many interviewers will look at when you are in an interview is your body language. The first one that will stand out is how you are sitting. Is your posture relaxed or is it so relaxed that you are slouching? Are you sitting in a way that makes it obvious that you are a professional and have respect for yourself or do you look like a high school freshman slouched down in the seat and barely awake?

They will also notice how you are holding your arms. Arms that are crossed across the chest are going to tell your interviewer that you are a closed book while open arms make you more approachable.

Many people will tap their foot, finger or click a pen when they are nervous, while many understand this is just something that people do, it can be distracting to the interviewer and may take their focus off of what you are saying. This, of course, means that when they sit back and think about the interview, all they are going to remember is the clicking of the pen.

Of course, while it is important that you make a great impression, it is okay for you to be nervous, and interviewers expect for you to be. However, it is important that you are not overly anxious, but instead that you are able to communicate with the interviewer just like you would with any other person. The interviewer wants you to be able to be yourself and not try to be something that you are not.

It is critical for you to look the interviewer in the eye. If your eyes are darting around the room, the interviewer might think that you are uncomfortable with their questions, or that you are bored with the interview.

The interviewer wants to make sure that you are also yourself. They want to ensure that you are not just giving them rehearsed lines, but that you are giving them spontaneous, true answers. They want to hear real stories of your experiences and see real emotions, such as excitement when you tell these stories.

It is important for you to show up prepared for the interview, ensuring that you know how you will answer common questions and that you know how you will highlight your successes. However, you should not only tell the interviewer what you think that he or she wants to know because this will make them feel that you are trying to hide something and that you are fake.

Some interviewers may try to get you to open up to them if they see that you have what they are looking for, but most are not going to go that far. To paint a great picture of yourself, you need to focus on the positives about yourself and the skills that you have. On the other hand, you should not make up skills or stories about yourself to get the job because even if the interviewer somehow does not see through it during the interview, it will become apparent when you start the job.

One of the most important things that an interviewer is looking for is your understanding of what the job actually is. It seems that many people are just applying for jobs without taking the time to understand what the job really is. When you apply for a position, you need to take some time to research the position as well as the company. You need to understand what will be expected of you, and what type of culture the company has. At the very least, you should take a few moments before the interview to reread the job description and make sure that you look up anything in the description that you are not familiar with.

The interviewer wants to know that you have taken the time to research the company. For example, if the company makes a certain line of products, the interviewer will want to know that you know what those products are. Simply doing a bit of research online about the company will give you all of the information you need, and it can even provide you with names of people that work at the company. Many interviewers will ask you what you know about the company, and it would be in favor for you to be able to answer that question.

It is imperative that the interviewer knows that you have the skills needed for the job. If for example, the position requires you to interact with a lot of people, someone with advanced public relations skills would be better suited for the position than someone that is shy or socially awkward. On the other hand, if the position is one that requires no social interaction, such as one that is done in a cubical, an extroverted person would not be a great fit because they would get bored.

Interviewers are also responsible for making sure that you will fit in with the culture of the company. There is really nothing you can do if you do not fit in with the culture of the company. You can give the best interview ever, you can answer all of the questions with well thought out answers, but there may be something that they know about the culture that you do not know, and you may not get the job. This does not mean that you have done something wrong; it simply means that you need to continue looking.

The interviewer wants to know that you are resourceful. While they are asking about your previous experiences, you are going to be telling them a lot of stories. What they are going to learn from these stories is whether or not you are a resourceful person and that you can think on your feet.

It is important for the interviewer to know that you are not high maintenance. There are really people out there who have complained during an interview because they have not been able to bring their parents with them, or they have called and emailed so many times that they have already gotten on the hiring manager's nerves before they have even had an interview. The interviewer can also tell if you are a high maintenance person by the way that you tell some of your stories. So, when you are practicing them, you want to make sure that you don't tell them in a way that makes you sound of high maintenance.

It is extremely important for you to be a problem solver, however; you need to make sure that you have all of the information before you begin trying to solve a problem. Some people think that they can try and solve a problem within a company before they have even been hired. There have been those that have taught people that if they come into an interview with some great idea of how to solve a problem within the company, they will be a shoe in for the job. However, no matter how much you think you know about the company, you cannot have all of the facts as an outsider, and the interviewer is actually going to look down on this.

If you want to show the interviewer that you are a problem solver, tell them stories about when you solved a problem at work in the past, but keep them short and to the point.

The interviewer wants to know that you are respectful to the management or others that are in charge. If you tell stories about your previous work experiences, and you are always putting down the former management or trying to make yourself look smarter than the management, it will not come across well to the interviewer It does not matter if the management was terrible at your previous job; it does not matter if you were smarter than everyone else in the entire company; you need to tell stories in a way that shows that you are resourceful, respectful and capable, but do so while not putting others down.

It is important for the interviewer to know that you are a self-starter. Respecting management is vital when it comes to any job, but that management needs to know that they are not going to have to micro-manage you. They need to know that when they are not looking, you are going to continue working and that they are not going to have to tell you every single thing that you have to do, every single minute of every single day.

The interviewer really wants to know that you are the type of person that can initiate change as well as a person that can handle change. One of the biggest complaints that you will find from many employees is that they are tired of the changes that are taking place within a company, they wish everything would just stay the same. While it is human nature to want things to remain stable, we have to understand that growth only happens through change, and we, as employees, should not fight against that change, but should accept it as well as initiate it. You can show that you are comfortable with change by telling stories of how you embraced it at a previous job.

We as people are far too complicated to paint an entire picture of ourselves in the few minutes that we have during an interview, and there really is no reason for you to try to do so. If you try to do this, you are going to come across as scattered and disconnected. Don't try to tell the interviewer everything there is to know about you in the few minutes that you have during an interview. Let your personality shine through during you interview, focus on the job, and let everyone get to know you once you have the job.

Take some time to review your resume before you go to the interview. It is very amazing how many times a potential employee is asked about something that is on their resume and they have no idea what the interviewer is talking about.

The interviewer wants to ensure what it would be like to work with you every day. Next to knowing if you are qualified to do the job, the interviewer wants to find out that you are going to be able to do your fair share of the work, and that you are going to be a positive addition to the company. They need to know that you are someone that can be relied on, that you can work well on a team, and that you can fill in where you are needed.

When you add all of these qualities together, the interviewer is able to find the perfect candidate for the job.

CHAPTER 9 - STRATEGIES FOR ANSWERING TOUGH QUESTIONS

. We all face tough questions during the interview process. For example, "What is your biggest weakness?" There are those that suggest that you should make light of the question and say something like "Ice cream" and there are those that advise you to flip the question around and focus on a positive aspect of yourself, such as "I'm a workaholic or perfectionist." However, you have to understand that what might work well for one person may not work well for the next.

While we are going to go over common questions as well as answers in a later chapter, there is no way for me to tell you the answer to every single question, but I can teach you how to respond to them.

The first thing that you need to know is that people love to hear stories. It is human nature to become interested in a story, and it is also human nature to want to tell these stories. So think about the question that is being asked or the story that is being requested. Then, create a short story that is going to highlight your accomplishments and make yourself look good, but tell the truth.

This brings us to the next topic, and that is honesty. You should always be honest when you are telling your stories or answering the questions. Answering honestly about yourself does not mean that you have to point out your worst flaws. For example, you do not need to tell the interviewer that you become angry with yourself when you are unable to do something. Even if this is you biggest flaw, you can word it so that it comes across as something positive, for example, "If I had to decide what my most significant flaw is, I would say that it is probably that I expect a lot more of myself than most people."

You see, you have focused on you in this statement instead of focusing on others or how a situation around you makes you feel. You have also turned what could be a negative aspect of yourself — getting upset when you cannot do something — to a positive one — expecting a lot of yourself. You have also been honest if this sentence reflects who you are.

You should not simply take answers from books that do not apply to you as a person and use them as your answers because once you start the job, the company is quickly going to find out that you are not the person that you portrayed yourself to be.

This type of answer also shows that you are not afraid to admit that you are not perfect, that you know you have flaws and can accept correction, but it indicates that the flaws that you do have are not that significant.

When an interviewer asks a person a question like this, they are looking to almost trick the person into honestly blurting out that they are lazy, or that they are late for work on a regular basis. This does happen, believe it or not, and this is how many interviewers weed out the bad apples in the bunch.

You should also make sure that you do not give any absolutes when you are answering questions. For example, in the above question, "What is your biggest flaw," you would say, "If I had to decide," not, "My biggest flaw is." If you also used the word "probably" to answer the above example that means this is not an absolute. An absolute means that there is no other answer, and this is exactly how it is. This is as huge of a mistake as it is to give a figure when the interviewer is asking you how much you expect to earn at the job because you could short yourself and no one wants to do that.

When you refuse to give absolutes in your answers, you allow yourself to focus on a positive aspect of yourself instead of something negative. You never want to focus on the negative. All of us have negative aspects of ourselves; we have negative thoughts and negative feelings, but we don't have to share those with the people around us and definitely not someone who is conducting an interview at a job we are trying to get.

It is also important for you to make sure that you understand the question and ask for clarification if it is needed. Of course, you don't have to sit there with a confused look on your face and say, "Huh," but merely repeat back to the interviewer what they said to you to ensure you understand what they want from you.

If the interviewer were to ask, "What is your biggest flaw," simply look back at them politely and repeat, "My biggest flaw." Of course, this is not a complicated question that needs a lot of clarification, but you get the point. Wait for a response, this will give you plenty of time to think about your answer. However, if it does not, you can still take a few seconds and think about what you need to say to make the best impression on the interviewer.

Then, begin the answer by restating what they asked, "I would probably say that my biggest flaw would be…" This shows the interviewer that you have listened to what was being asked and that you are giving the question some thought instead of spouting off the first thing that comes to your mind or providing them with some rehearsed answer.

It is also vitally important when it comes to answering the questions that you remain calm. If you are not calm, you are not going to be able to think clearly, your voice is going to be shaking, and you are not going to be able to give an appropriate response in the short amount of time that the interviewer has to spend with you.

While the interviewer does have a limited amount of time to spend with you in the interview, you do not want to rush your answers. If you rush to reply to the questions, you may say something that you later wish you had not, you may not answer the question appropriately, or you may just come across as someone that wants to get out of the interview as soon as possible; someone that does not take the process seriously.

When you are giving your answers, you want to be specific, and you want to use your response to focus on the job that you are applying for. For example, when asked what your greatest strength is, you should choose something that is of high value to that specific company. This is why it is crucial that you take the time to research a company before you go to the interview. You need to be able to match up your characteristics with what they need in the company.

Take for example, if you have researched and find that this specific company that you want to work for has had a lot of accidents in the past few months, and you have a lot of workplace safety training. If you did not do the research, you would not know that you have a skill that is of high value to that company right then.

This, of course, means that you should inform the interviewer of your accomplishments through your answers. You never know if your accomplishments will inspire the interviewer about a skill that you have which will help the company and put you in the front running for the position.

Many interviewers will ask you about your accomplishments because they want to know what you have done in the past. You should not feel as if you are boasting or that they will think you are trying to look good only because you tell them about these accomplishments. Even if they do not ask, it is important to highlight them in your answers to ensure they have as much information about you as possible which will make it easier for them to decide that they want to hire you.

When you discuss your accomplishments, you need to focus on workplace accomplishments. Unless you are applying for your first job, no one cares that you were the president of a club in high school or that you got a poem published. Just stick to accomplishments that pertain to the job you are applying for.

It is also important that when you are answering these questions, you do not ramble. Stay focused on the question that was asked, make sure that your answers focus on the job that you are applying for, and always ensure that you do not get off topic. If the interviewer asks questions that are off topic, and the two of you begin to talk, that is great. It simply shows that the interviewer is connecting with you. However, you should never be the person that veers off topic during an interview.

It is understandable that this may seem like it is going to be very difficult to do, because as you have read this chapter, you probably think that this is not how we as humans typically answer questions that are presented to us, and that is true. Therefore, it is essential that you take the time to practice answering questions in this manner before you go to any interview.

You have to remember that you are not going to have a cheat sheet sitting in front of you telling you how to answer the questions properly. You are going to have to answer all of these questions from memory, and if you try to remember everything that you have learned about answering questions in this chapter, you are going to become overwhelmed, and the interview is not going to go very well.

You can practice alone or have someone practice with you by giving them the list of the 50 most common interview questions that we will go over later in this book. Having them ask you a few of them at a time, allowing you to prepare yourself by answering real interview questions and getting used to coming up with great answers.

I NEED YOUR HELP

I really want to thank you again for reading this book. Hopefully you have liked it so far and have been receiving value from it. Lots of effort was put into making sure that it provides as much content as possible to you and that I cover as much as I can.

If you've found this book helpful, then I'd like to ask you a favor. Would you be kind enough to leave a review for it on Amazon? It would be greatly appreciated!

CHAPTER 10 - HOW NOT TO ANSWER A QUESTION

While we discussed in the last chapter how you should answer a question, I feel that it is vital for you to know what you should not do as well. Not only how you should not answer a question but what you should not do in the interview itself, and that is where I want to begin.

Of course, there are specific things that you can do and say during an interview that can cost you your chance at the job. Some of these seem very obvious to some while not so obvious to others, so let's take a few minutes and discuss them before moving on to how not to answer a question.

The first thing that you do not want to do when it comes to your interview is dress inappropriately. We will go over how you should dress for an interview in a later chapter, but this needs to be thought of ahead of time, and you need to make sure that you do not go into an interview simply wearing your street clothes because this will not give the interviewer a good impression of you.

Second, you NEVER arrive late. When the first thing that you have to say to a potential employer is, "Sorry I'm late," chances are, you are not going to get the job. Unless you have been abducted by aliens, you should arrive at the interview about 15 minutes early just to ensure that you are not late. When you do this, you are going to show the interviewer that you are punctual and that they are going to be able to depend on you to arrive to work on time every day.

When you arrive at the interview, you absolutely have to be polite to the receptionist as well as any other employee that you come into contact with. NEVER be rude to anyone that works at the company. While this may seem like common sense, it is a mistake that many people make. You have to understand that most companies are fairly tight knit. This means that if you are rude to even the janitor, they will let the hiring manager know what you have done ensuring that you have absolutely no chance at getting the job. Even if you do still get the job, they are going to let everyone in the company know just how you treated them, ensuring that you are not well accepted into the company. You also need to remember that you have no idea who you are being rude to. It might just be the owner's wife sitting at that receptionist desk.

Do not look at, fidget with or answer your phone while you are in the middle of an interview. You should not even have your phone on, and if it must be on, it should be on silent, allowing you to focus all of your attention on the interview. Trust me, if your child is sick at school, the nurse will leave a message, and you can call her back 15 minutes later when the interview is over. However, if you pick up that phone, tell the interviewer that it is your child's school; they are going to assume that this type of thing happens a lot, and it is likely that you will not get the job.

Another mistake that many people make when they go to an interview is that they do not shake the interviewer's hand, nor do they look the interviewer in the eyes when they speak. It is understandable that it is not comfortable for everyone to look people in the eyes, especially if you are the introverted type. However, you can get around this by looking at the space between the person's eyes, and they will be none the wiser. Keeping your head down or looking around the room while they speak or while you answer questions is going to make you look a bit scatter brained or uninterested in the position. It is also going to bring up concerns when it comes to training you for the job, the interviewer may think that you do not have a long enough attention span to actually learn the work or do the work.

In a later chapter, we are going to talk a lot about some of the questions that you should ask the interviewer during the interview, but another mistake is that many people don't take the time to prepare or even ask these questions. Or, they begin asking questions about pay, vacation time, or other benefits before they ever get the job. Some people have even been known to ask that the work day is scheduled around their life, for example, asking if they can come in an hour later than everyone else because they have some sort of obligation. These questions are not interview questions; these questions should be discussed after you already have the job offer. You should always show up at the interview with at least three questions that you need answers to which will help you make an informed decision if you are offered the job.

Never let the interviewer know that this is not really the job that you want, but that you are willing to accept it if you do not get the job that you want. No one wants to be someone's second choice, and no interviewer wants to think that the company they are representing was not your first choice. Be as excited and energetic about this interview as you were with the first choice job and then make your decision when you find out which job or jobs are offered to you. You don't want to state that you are waiting for another company to call you before you decide where you want to work because you may blow your chances at getting a call from the second company by doing this.

I have stated it several times, but it is of vital importance that you go into an interview having done some research about the company. Most of the time, the interviewer, is going to ask you what you know about the company. Never go into an interview and tell them that you did not have the time or did not take the time to research the company and that you really do not know anything about it. You have to remember that the person that is interviewing you loves the company that they work for. Now, if you could not take 15 minutes out of your day to look at the company's website and learn a little bit, it is quite insulting to them, and it shows that you are not actually interested in the company, but that you just want a job.

Do not use text talk or slang while you are in an interview. This is one mistake that many people make without even thinking about it. We have become so used to using slang that we, as a society, rarely even notice when we are doing it, but you have to save the slang for outside of the interview and present yourself as a professional during the interview process. There is no awesome sauce in an interview, no matter how excited you get. You should take some time and practice speaking professionally. This may seem awkward at first, but it gets much easier with practice, and you will find that after a few sessions of practice, it comes naturally to you.

When you are in an interview, as well as while you are on the job, you need to present yourself as a professional. It does not matter what you act like outside of work, as long as it does not affect your job, but you need to remember that when you walk through the doors of any business you are applying to, or you are working at, you are a professional, and you want people to see you that way.

One huge mistake that some people make when they arrive at an interview is that they feel the need to announce that they are hungover. This is a big no-no, and you really should not even go to an interview when you are hungover. First, you don't have to announce it, the interviewer can already tell and what you are showing them is that you do not take the interview seriously, not that you are some hip, fun person with a great social life. Second, you are showing the interviewer that it is likely that you will be showing up for work hungover. This is not the impression that you want to make because you are not going to get the job this way. It would be better for you to cancel the interview altogether, telling them that a giant asteroid hit your car than to show up hungover. (Do not tell them that a giant asteroid hit your car.)

It is natural for you to be curious about the number of hours that you are going to be working each week, but you should not bring this up during the interview, for example, stating that your friend told you that most people work more than 40 hours a week. The fact is, no matter where you work, most people work more than 40 hours per week. It is how we live life today. Bringing this up while you are in the interview is going to give the impression that you are a clock watcher, that you are there only to earn a paycheck, and that you are not going to be willing to put in the extra effort that is needed to make the company run smoothly.

Never bring attention to the fact that you are not qualified for the job. Even if you lack some experience, it does not matter. Remember when I said that you have to focus on the positive aspects and avoid the negative ones? This is a negative one. Bringing this to their attention may make them rethink hiring you even if they were ready to offer you the job before you mentioned your lack of qualifications. So many jobs are landed by people who are not qualified because they aced the interview. The interviewer believes that while they are not currently qualified for the job they can learn it. You have to remember that no one that applies for the job is exactly what the interviewer is looking for, and drawing attention to your flaws may make them rethink hiring you.

I have said this before, but I believe that it is very essential that we go over it again. NEVER during the interview process talk poorly about your previous bosses. We have all had them, bosses that should have never been given the position, bosses who had no idea how to be bosses, but you do not have to share this with the interviewer. You should not tell them that your previous boss was a complete jerk that picked on you. You shouldn't even tell them that the two of you did not see eye to eye. Remember, keep it positive even if you could not stand to look at your previous boss.

The bottom line is that if you want to avoid all of the mistakes that most people make when they arrive at an interview, be professional and positive. By doing those two things, you will find that your interview goes smoothly, and you are getting more callbacks than ever before.

Now I want to spend a few moments talking about how to not answer a question while you are in an interview.

When you are answering a question in an interview you do not want to give the interviewer a generic answer. Instead, you need to provide vivid examples, referring to the organization as well as yourself, making sure that the answer does not sound as if it has been prepared. An example of this would be if asked why you applied for the company, a generic answer might be that you are interested in the type of work the company does. A good answer would be, "Through a hobby of mine, I became quite interested in the company. My interest has grown over the years, and now I feel that the next step is to join the company." That is the type of answer that will get you a job offer.

Do not try to be a politician – unless that is what you are trying to be. Not giving a straight answer is one of the worst things that you can do during a job interview. If you are unsure of what is being requested of you, then ask. If you are unsure if you answered the question, state that or ask if there is anything that you left out.

Interviewers are notorious for asking 15 questions before you can get one answered, so do not feel as if you have to answer them all at the same time. Take a breath, answer one question, and then ask what the next question was. They do not expect for you to be able to remember all of them, and in fact, some of them are just testing you to see what you will do.

Answering a question before taking the time to think about the question as well as your answer is another common mistake. This is what many interviewers are counting on when they ask questions such as, "What is your biggest flaw." They are hoping to catch you off guard and that you will provide them with some information that will knock you out of the running for the job. Not only this, but if you don't think about the question as well as your answer, you could end up giving an answer that has nothing to do with the question that was asked. This is going to make you look as if you do not listen, which is a vital skill for any job.

When people are answering questions, it is a common mistake for them to provide very long answers. While this may seem like the right way to go, it really is not. You have to remember that you are not the only person that this interviewer has seen that day, the chances are that they have listened to people ramble on for most of the day, and they really don't want to do it again. You should not give one-word answers either; you should keep them short and to the point. If you know that you have more information that the interviewer might be interested in knowing, simply tell them that if they need to know more, you can provide the details for them. Your answers should take from 20 seconds to a minute and no more unless the interviewer asks you for more details.

While it is important for you to understand that the interviewer is there to do their job, and they do have more people to see, it is also important for you to quickly connect with the interviewer and have some conversation. You have to build some rapport. If all that you are doing is answering questions, you are not going to create rapport so you can use those questions to create a conversation between you and the interviewer. For example, if the interviewer were to ask you to tell them about some of the challenges you have faced and how you overcame them, you would answer the question and then ask what some of the challenges are that employees at the company have to face. This will not only show that you are interested in the job, but it will get the conversation going and help you to decide if this is the right job for you.

Interview questions can be tough, and it is easy to make mistakes. However, when you answer the questions firmly and appropriately, you are going to leave a great impression and increase your chances of getting offered the job.

CHAPTER 11 - 25 COMMON QUESTIONS AND HOW TO ANSWER THEM

There was a time when offbeat questions were becoming the norm when it came to an interview. When you would be asked to describe the color purple to a person that was blind or why a manhole cover is a circle instead of a square. However, research has found that these questions really do not help to predict how a person will perform on the job, whereas it was once thought that they would allow the interviewer to understand how the person would work under pressure, and if they would be able to think outside of the box.

What has been found, however, is that nothing more was gained from these questions than the boost of confidence that the interviewer got from asking them. Because of this, most companies are aborting the habit of asking these types of questions, which is excellent news for people who are trying to prepare for an interview.

In this chapter, I want to go over the 50 most common interview questions as well as how you should answer them. By practicing these questions and preparing your answers, you will guarantee that you are ready for your interview no matter which questions the interviewer chooses to ask.

Why should I hire you?

This is a very common question, and it is one that often makes people stumble over their words. To answer this question, you do not want to just list off all of the experience or accomplishments that you have on your resume, the interviewer is already aware of these. Instead, you should provide them with a real answer that tells them why they should hire you. What do you have to offer to the company that makes you a better hire than anyone else that they have interviewed? A good answer would be: I believe that I would be an asset to this company because I have the skills that you are looking for; I am able to work autonomously, I have great communication skills as well as strong leadership skills.

Don't you think that you are overqualified for this job?

While you may find that you are overqualified for some of the jobs that you apply to, you need to make it clear to the interviewer that you are not using the company as just a placeholder until a better job is offered to you by another company. You want to make them understand that you want to work for them. You can do this by telling them that as you have grown older, you are no longer concerned with titles, but instead want to work in a job that makes you feel happy and fulfilled and that this position will do just that. Really explain to them why you want to work for that company, besides the check that you will be getting at the end of the week.

Tell me about a difficult work experience and how you handled it.

There is not going to be a right or wrong answer to this question. What the interviewer is wanting to see by asking you this question is that when you are faced with a challenging experience that you are able to handle it. They are also looking to find out what type of decision you feel is a difficult one. The best way for you to answer this question is to give one or two examples of difficult work experiences that you have had to deal with in the past and talk about how you were able to handle each one. Only talk about those experiences that you handled in a professional manner and that you were successful at handling. You want to make sure that the interviewer sees you as confident, and as someone that is able to make hard decisions.

Tell me about yourself.

Many interviewers will start with this question because it is an ice breaker. It is a way to make you feel comfortable and to help you open up and talk to them. It is also a great way for the interviewer to understand a bit about your personality which will help them when it comes to deciding if you are the right fit for the job.

Some people jump right into this question by listing all of their accomplishments, their skills, and previous work experience. Do not do this if you want the job. This is your time to build a bit of rapport with the interviewer and give him or her a little peak into your life. Tell them a bit about some of the hobbies you are interested in, talk about the volunteer work that you do, talk about how much you love to run in the mornings, how you are involved in the community or about the last fundraiser you took part in.

Show them your skills by discussing your interests and opening up to them a little bit. Believe it or not, I have received many job offers simply because of one specific hobby that I have. You never know what it is that is going to make an interviewer choose you above someone else so when they ask you to tell them about yourself, do it.

Tell me about your best boss… as well as your worst.

This is a trick question and should be answered very carefully. The interviewer is trying to determine if you are the type of person that carries a grudge, or if you are the type that lays blame on other people. Even if you had the worst boss in the world, do not tell this to the interviewer. I have stated several times in this book that you should never badmouth your previous boss, and many people know this, but when they are asked this question, they think it is a green flag to go ahead and do so. It is not. Instead, simply say something like, "Each one of my previous bosses taught me so much it would be difficult to choose a best. There were times that were challenging, but I am grateful for everything that I learned from all of them."

What are your career goals?

Many interviewers ask this question or one similar to it because they are trying to assess if you are self-aware or not, and they are trying to determine if you have any long term goals for yourself in your career. They want to know if the company you are applying to is going to fit in with your career goals. They need to know that you are planning on staying with the company for a long time because it does cost the company money to continually train new employees. They would prefer to have an employee that is going to stay with the company than one that is going to bounce from one company to another.

You can begin answering this question by discussing what your short-term goals are, then move on to your long-term goals. Talk about the steps that you will have to take to reach the goals that you have set for yourself, focus on how the company fits in with your short-term as well as your long-term goals, but it is important that you not get too specific. For example, if the company that you are interviewing with is just a stepping stone to help you reach your goals, it is not a good idea to share that with the interviewer nor is it a good idea to tell them that you see yourself working at another company in the next five years.

How would you describe your work style?

This question is most commonly asked as a way to assess if you would fit in with the culture of the company as well as to assess self-awareness. If you are not self-aware enough to describe the way that you work to the interviewer, chances are, they are not going to consider you for the job. They want to hire someone that understands what they need to complete a job. When you are answering this question, you need to avoid telling the interviewer that you are a good communicator or that you are a hard worker. Instead, focus on what is going to fit within the company that you are applying to.

For example, focus on how quickly you work and how accurate your work is. Let the interviewer know that you produce quality work very quickly and that you can meet deadlines without a problem.

Explain to the interviewer that you are the type of person that does the hardest jobs at the beginning of the day to get them done and that you never put them off until later. Let the interviewer know that you are the type of person that goes above and beyond the call of duty and that you are willing to work as hard as you need to in order to get the job done.

It is also important that the interviewer understands that you are able to take direction when it is given to you, but that you do not need to be given direction constantly.

While all of this may seem like it is leading to a very complex and lengthy answer, it is important for you to remember to keep your answers short and that you stay on point when answering the questions.

Do you like to work alone or do you prefer to work on a team?

This is another one of those questions that may feel as if it is a tricky question because we all know that there are specific times that we want to work alone as well as specific projects that we want to work on a team. However, understanding that you are going to be a part of a company means that you have to be able to work on a team as well. It is for this reason that some people stare blankly at their interviewer unable to answer this question when it is asked.

The interviewer is asking this question because he or she needs to know that you are able to work on your own, often with little supervision, but they also want to know that you are open to working with a team and being part of a team.

Highlighting the fact that you are able to do both is going to increase your chances of getting offered the job dramatically. Explain that you see the benefits of both, that there are times when you feel that it is best to work alone, and there are times that you feel it is best to work as a team. Also stating that even when you are working alone, you know that you really are working as part of the team that makes up the company is a great way to reassure the interviewer that you know the importance of teamwork.

However, you need to be very careful when you are answering this question because if you are the type of person that works best when you are alone, you do not want to tell the interviewer that you work best when you are on a team because it could backfire, and you could end up stuck with a job that is on a team. To avoid this, simply state that you enjoy working on a team sometimes, but you feel that you do your best work when you are alone.

Some interviewers will ask if you normally take your work home with you, and this can be a very tricky question. Some interviewers are going to want to know if you regularly take work home because they are trying to find out if you are able to get the work done during the hours you are allotted each day. Many employers today believe that it is important for their employees to have a good work-life balance because studies have shown that this leads to happier employees that work harder for the company.

On the other hand, there are still companies out there that want you to make the company and your work the main focus of your life, which means in this case, they would want you to take your work home with you.

To answer this question, you are going to have to think about the culture of the company. It is going to be up to you to decide if the company is the kind that wants to ensure that you are the type of person that has a balanced life or the type of person that will make the company the center of their life. If you are part of a company that wants the company to be the most important factor in your life, then you need to be sure that you are willing to make it the most important factor in your life.

Some interviewers might also ask you to give them some examples of teamwork. This is a great way for an interviewer to determine how well a potential employee will work with others. It is important for employers to hire people who are team players and that means that you need to answer in a way that shows that you are a team player.

Very few jobs that you will ever do in your life are done without teamwork, so it should not be too difficult for you to come up with a few examples of teamwork. Talk about a time when you worked on a team to solve a problem at a previous job or a time that you worked on a team to complete a project. Tell the interviewer about your role on the team and make sure that you mention the outcome. While you are talking about teamwork, avoid talking too much about 'I'. I did this… I was in charge of this… I came up with this… And so on. Make sure you talk about 'we,' as in you and your team.

1. Getting asked if you have ever had a problem with a manager or another boss is a question that is asked during a lot of interviews. It is important to know how to answer this question because if you answer it wrong, you may come across as someone that has a problem with authority and it can cost you your job.
2. Most of us have had a problem boss or manager at one point or another in our lives. We all know that not all people who are in a position of authority know how to handle it, but during an interview is not the time to talk about it.
3. The reason that interviewers ask this is that they want to know that you are a team player and that you do not have a problem taking direction from those who are in a position of authority.

4. The interviewer does not want to hear all about how you have had problems with a previous boss. In fact, they do not want to hear anything negative about one of your former bosses at all. This is another one of those questions that the interviewer will ask in an attempt to trip you up and get you to confess something that you know you should not be telling them.

5. Anger is also an issue that may be brought up, some interviewers will ask if you have ever been angry at work, and they will want to know what happened. They may ask you when the last time that you got angry was and ask you what happened. When the interviewer talks about anger, they are not talking about the last time you got upset, they are talking about the last time you lost control.

6. The interviewer is asking this question because they want to understand how well you deal with a difficult situation. They also are trying to find out if you are able to maintain your professionalism while you are dealing with a difficult situation.

7. The first thing that you need to know when answering this question is that you need to avoid intense emotional words such as anger, angry or hate. Instead, you can use words like disappointed and frustrated. You want to make sure that it is understood that you did NOT lose control in the situation and that you remained professional. Do not spend your time blaming the other people involved in the situation. Simply mention what is was that upset you and what you did to deal with the problem.

8. Since it is important for the interviewer to know how well you handle pressure, they may simply come out and ask you. When you are asked how you react when you are under pressure or how you handle being under pressure or stress, the interviewer is not looking for you to tell them that you do not have stress.

9. We all know that everyone feels stressed at some point, and the interviewer is simply trying to find out what your reaction to the stress would be. However, you do not want your response to be negative. The interviewer is simply trying to determine if you handle stress in a positive or negative way, therefore, you should try to focus on something productive that you do when you are stressed. For example, you could tell the interviewer that when you find yourself dealing with a lot of stress, you spend some time cleaning to clear your mind. Or that you take a step back away from what is stressing you out and come back to it later to figure it out with a clear mind.

10. How would you measure success? This is a question that

interviewers ask because they want to know that you do not measure success in the form of dollars.

11. This question is going to let the interviewer know a bit about your personality, how you feel about life, and your business ethic. Everyone knows that money is important; that is why we work, but there is also another part of us that works because we want to be successful. That may mean that you enjoy your job, that you are proud of what you do or that you spend a certain amount of time with your family or a million other things. When you answer this question, don't focus on money. Focus on something else in your life that makes you feel successful.

12. You may be asked how long you expect to work for the company if you are offered the job. I mentioned earlier that the interviewer wants to ensure that this job is not just going to be a placeholder for you until a better job comes along and this is just another way for them to ensure that.

13. If you tell the interviewer that you only plan on being in the position for a short amount of time, you will likely remove yourself from the list of potential employees. Even if you do not plan on being with the company for a long period of time, it is important to let the interviewer know that the company is not going to be losing money by hiring you. I mentioned earlier that companies spend a lot of money to train their employees, and they want to ensure that their money is not going to be wasted.

14. If you do not plan on staying with the company for a long period of time, focus on how the company fits in with your goals, the great aspects of the company, and why you want to work for them.

15. How much are you expecting to get paid? This is a common question that interviewers ask, but before you start talking about money with the interviewer, it is important for you to know how much the job is worth.

16. This is one of the reasons that it is very important for you to do your research before you go to an interview. If you give the interviewer a number that is too small, they may agree to it, and you will cost yourself the money. On the other hand, if you give them a number that is too high, it could cost you the job.

17. What is your work pace like? Your answer to this question is going to depend greatly on the job. However, steady is always a great answer no matter where you are applying. If you are applying to a company that you know has a fast paced work environment, then you need to make sure that you are able to work at that pace and that you will enjoy working at that pace.

18. Many interviewers will ask you to describe yourself, and this can take you off guard because while it may seem simple sitting in your living room, however, when you get in front of an interviewer it is not as simple as it seems.

19. The interviewer is asking you this because they want to know if you are going to fit in with the company's culture. To prepare for this question, take a few moments to sit down with your friends and family asking them what words they would use to describe you. Choose three to five of these that you feel that best fit you and use them when you are asked to describe yourself.

20. What do you do if your boss is wrong?

21. This is a question that can make your air catch in your throat because you want to make a good impression, but you do not want to seem as if you think that you are right all of the time. The simple way to answer this question is to tell the interviewer that you would talk to your boss alone, explaining why you feel that they are wrong. Explain that you think it is rare for a boss to be wrong and do not speak poorly about a previous boss that was wrong.

22. If I were to ask your closest three friends why I should hire you, what would they say?

23. This is a bit of an off the wall question, but believe it or not, it is one that gets asked during many interviews. This is basically a different way of asking you why they should hire you and to answer this question, you need to give them an honest answer. Are you dedicated? Are you a hard worker? Are you a fast learner? These all can be used as answers as well as any other POSITIVE reasons why you think that you should get the job. You should, however, not tell the interviewer that they will not find anyone else as qualified, dedicated or hard working as you because they will ensure that they do so, and you will never get the chance to prove them wrong.

24. What type of work environment do you prefer?

25. Hopefully, you took some time to do some research about the work environment of the company before you applied for the job or at least before you decided to show up for the interview so this should give you a little bit of information that will help you answer this question.

26. The only thing that the interviewer is trying to figure out by asking this question is if you will fit in with the company culture, and they are trying to understand what environment helps to ensure that you will be the most productive. If you

have not been able to find out about the company culture through research, it is okay for you to take a few moments and ask about the environment of the company as well as the culture.

27. Why do you want to work here? Or, why did you choose to apply to this company?

28. The answer to this question is going to vary from person to person. I spoke earlier about how I received several job offers simply because I applied to companies that had to do with one of my favorite hobbies. I already know what went on within the company and the policies because I had become such a fan of it through my hobby. I also believed that my hobby would make me an asset to the company.

29. You want to provide a meaningful answer. Do not just tell the interviewer that it was the only company hiring for the position that you wanted or that you don't know why you want to work for the company or that you just want a paycheck. None of these are going to help you to get the job. What you do want to do, however, is to make sure that you personalize your answer. Show the interviewer that even though you are not part of the company yet, that you care about the company, that you want to see it succeed, and that you are willing to do whatever it takes to ensure the company's success.

30. Tell me what you are passionate about.

31. This question is asked by the interviewer to determine whether or not you are a dedicated person if you are well-rounded and to see if you have a life outside of work. The interviewer wants to see that you are not afraid to try new things, but that you stick to the old things that you enjoy instead of quitting everything that you try.

32. There is no right or wrong answer to this question. Simply tell the interviewer about the things that you are passionate about and don't try to make up things simply to impress the interviewer because when a person talks about something that they are passionate about, they become excited, and you can hear the passion in their voice. This type of passion cannot be faked so just be honest.

33. What is your biggest accomplishment in life as well as your biggest failure?

34. Many people will tell the interviewer that their biggest accomplishment is their children, and that is fine if you move on to the next biggest accomplishment quickly. The interviewer wants to know more about the accomplishments that you have

had in your career, not in your personal life while it is okay to mention a few here and there, this question focuses on your career.

35. This is a great place for you to tell a story and make a connection with the interviewer. When it comes to describing your biggest failure, you have to be careful because if you state that you don't know your biggest failure, it is going to be apparent that you are not self-aware. However, if you provide the interviewer with some huge failure like the felony that you committed last year and didn't get caught doing, you will cost yourself the job.

36. Some people will tell you that if you have not failed, then you should tell the interviewer that despite that is going to make you look arrogant. If you cannot think of a failure in your life, simply tell them that you do not think of failure in the same way that most people do, that instead, you believe that failure only exists if you give up and that you will never give up.

37. When can you start? This is the question that all of us want to hear, but it is also an important one. If you are unemployed, simply make sure that you have no other arrangements that need to be taken care of such as doctor's appointments and then give your start date. If, on the other hand, you are still employed, you need to let the interviewer know when your two weeks' notice is up, and that you will be able to start after that date.

38. This is important because you want the interviewer to know that you are not just going to walk out on the job that you already have, because, remember, past behaviors often predict future behaviors, and that interviewer does not want you to leave that company without giving any notice.

39.

There are a lot of questions that can be asked during an interview, but most of the questions that you are going to be asked are simply the same questions that you have learned about in this chapter. However, they are worded just a bit differently. This is why even when you practice your responses that it is vital for you to listen carefully to the question that is being asked.

CHAPTER 12 - QUESTIONS YOU NEED TO ASK. INTERVIEW THE INTERVIEWER.

Many people forget when they are in a job interview that this is your time to interview the interviewer to determine if this really is a company that they want to work for. You have to remember that while the interviewer did call you in to interview you, you also have the right to ask as many questions as you need to in order to ensure that you are making a well-informed decision.

It is for that reason that I want to spend just a moment on a few questions that you need to make sure that you know the answer to before you leave the job interview.

You don't have to worry about interrupting the interviewer in hopes of getting the answers to your questions because at the end of the interview you will be asked if you have any questions. Simply smile, nod your head and say, "Yes I do."

1. It is important for you to ask how employees learn as well as how they develop while they are working at the company. The reason for this is because we all want to move up in the companies we work for, we want to learn new stuff, and we don't want to be stuck doing the same job for the next 20 years. However, it is also important because you know how you learn better than anyone else and if you find that this specific company teaches through videos and tests while you are more of a hands-on learning type of person, you might want to consider that this job is not for you.

2. What is the performance review process like? This is another good question that you will want to talk to the interviewer about because it is important that you know if you are going to have formal reviews or more casual ones. This question might

also help the interviewer to open up about what is required by a person that would hold a similar position to the one that you are applying to. This, of course, will let you know whether or not you want the job, or if you want to keep waiting for the next one to call.

3. You need to take a few moments after an offer has been made to ensure that it fits your needs. It is best if you already have this planned out. You should sit down with a pen and paper, figure out what your bills are and how much money you need to earn to survive. Keep this figure with you because it is going to help you when you are in the job interview process. If someone tries to lowball you, not offering enough money for you to live off of, you know that you can walk away and pick up the next job that comes your way, and that will pay the type of money that you need.

4. This question is not just about money, though, you need to think about medical insurance, dental, vision, retirement plans, stock purchasing and all of the other benefits that might come along with the job. If the job does not provide you with the benefits that you need, then you probably should consider moving on to the next job on your list.

5. Why is there an opening for this position? You need to understand exactly why this position is open. Did someone retire? Did someone move on to a larger company? Did someone quit because there was too much responsibility placed on their shoulders?

6. There are millions of reasons why a person might leave a job, and you can speculate all that you want, but you are never going to know the truth unless you ask. If you ask and you do not like the answer, it is no big deal because you have not accepted the offer, which means that you are not stuck with a job that you are going to hate.

CHAPTER 13 - WHAT YOU NEED TO LET THE INTERVIEWER KNOW

.

While you are going to have questions for the interviewer, there are also a few things that you need to make sure you let the interviewer know. The first thing that comes to mind when I think about what you need to tell the interviewer about is doctor, dentist or vision appointments.

Most companies are fairly relaxed when it comes to working around a new person's old schedule. They understand that you have probably had these appointments for six months, and they do not want to make you continue to wait while you begin a new job. However, you do need to make sure that you not only let the interviewer know about this... after you have had the job offer, but that you let your floor manager know as well.

It is also vital that you tell the interviewer if you require any special arrangements due to a disability. It is illegal for a company not to hire you because of a disability however it is not illegal for them to fire you if you did not divulge this information before you were offered the job.

When you are offered the job, you also need to tell the interviewer of any specific days that you need off as well as the times that you are available to work. Of course, this should already be on your resume or application. However, it is also a good idea to simply remind them of this to ensure that you do not get stuck scheduled on the weekends if that is something you cannot do.

CHAPTER 14 - HOW TO DRESS FOR AN INTERVIEW

. Dressing for your interview is critical. The way that you dress for your interview is going to be what the interviewer's first impression is made off of. That and if you arrived earlier or late for the interview.

You need to dress for the job that you are applying for. For example, if you are going to apply to work at a factory as a production worker, do not wear a suit and tie. However, if you are applying to work in an office setting, you need to make sure that you wear office attire.

Make sure that your clothes are not wrinkled and that they do not smell of mildew. Many people do not wear their 'interview' clothes on a regular basis and forget that they can collect all sorts of smells while hanging in the closet so make sure that they get a good washing.

You should also make sure that your shoes are clean and in good condition. Never go to an interview with your toe sticking out the top of your shoe or the sole falling off. This will give the interviewer a terrible impression because they will feel that if you do not have enough respect to dress properly for the interview, you are not taking the job seriously.

It is also important that you keep jewelry down to a minimum. Take out any facial jewelry that you might have; women should only wear one small set of earrings, nothing too flashy and a small necklace if desired. You should not go to an interview covered in costume jewelry.

You also need to pay close attention to the amount of makeup that you are wearing if you are a woman. You do not want to go into an interview with a distracting amount of makeup caked onto your face, but instead want to keep it fresh and simple.

The same thing is true when it comes to the amount of perfume or cologne that you wear. You do not want it to be overpowering, and it is really best if you do not wear any at all because the interviewer could be allergic and that will not make for a good interview. Instead, use a bit of lightly scented lotion, the smell is not overpowering, and it will not cause the interviewer to begin sneezing their head off as soon as you walk into the room.

CHAPTER 15 - WHAT TO DO AFTER AN INTERVIEW

Knowing what you should do after an interview is just as important as knowing what to do during the interview. If you are not offered the job on the spot and believe me that does happen a lot, you are going to need to take some time to follow up.

Some people will tell you that you should send a thank you card or letter in the mail, thanking the company for their time and clearing up any mistakes in answers that you may have made. However, I do not agree with this. This type of behavior will make you seem desperate.

The first thing that you need to do if you do not get hired right away is to ask the interviewer when you can expect to hear from him or her. Then mark this date on your calendar. Continue taking other interviews and looking for a job while you wait for the call.

If the date comes and you find that the interviewer has not called you back, then it is time to start making calls. Call the company, tell them that you had an interview and that you had not heard back, and you wanted to check to see if the position had been filled.

Let them know that you are still interested in the position and go from there. At this point, you might be transferred to human resources or called in for another interview. You may also be told that the date was pushed back.

What you do not want to do is start calling the company the day after the interview and hounding them for a job. This is going to frustrate them before you are ever offered the job, and it is going to lower your chances of finally getting it.

If you are offered the job and the managers tell you that he or she will call you with your schedule when it is ready, do not continue to hound them asking for your schedule.

You have to remember that you are not the only person that they are dealing with on a day to day basis. However, when you hound them, bug them, and try to get a call back before they are ready, you may as well not even have gone to the interview because this type of behavior will cost you your job. At the very least, it is going to upset the manager that you are calling and quickly put you on their bad side.

The truth is if you have followed all of the tips in this book, if you have conducted your interview appropriately and answered the questions the way that I have suggested, you do not have to worry about not getting called back. If there is a second interview, you will get it, and if you have completed your interview successfully, you might as well accept that the job is in the bag.

There is no reason for you to pace the floor for a week while you are waiting for the phone call. Get on with your life; keep applying for other jobs. If you accept one and another one calls, it is no big deal, simply tell them you are no longer looking.

Then, when the phone rings and you get the message that you got the job, you will really be able to enjoy it because you will know that you did not waste any time stressing out about something that was out of your hands at that point.

CONCLUSION

I hope this book was able to help you achieve success while applying for your dream job. It's definitely a nerve-racking thing to go into an interview where you will be judged and scrutinized. Just remember to try your best at everything you do, and you will surely succeed. Success isn't something that comes easy. However, with a little hard work and determination, it is most definitely possible.

The next step is to take what you've learned from this book, make sure you know it inside and out, and go get yourself the job you've always wanted!

Thanks again for buying this book and good luck!

RELATED READING

I have the perfect complement to this book on job interviewing to further help you with your career goals. In order to be as successful as you can at getting a job you need to make sure you get as many interviews as possible. The best way to do this is by creating a killer resume. You need a resume that will make potential employers want to hire you before they even meet you.

I highly recommend you check out my book, '*The Winning Resume 2nd Ed. – Get Hired Today with These Groundbreaking Resume Secrets*'. It is available on Amazon in paperback and digital format.

CPSIA information can be obtained
at www.ICGtesting.com
Printed in the USA
LVOW13s1817130217
524117LV00010B/1105/P